Encounters

Encounters
Inspiration from the Natural World

Poetry by Nan Rubin

Encounters: Inspiration from the Natural World

Published by Wheatmark®
1760 East River Road, Suite 145
Tucson, Arizona 85718 USA
www.wheatmark.com

ISBN: 978-1-62787-378-9
LCCN: 2015959765

It is the marriage of the soul with Nature that makes the intellect fruitful, and gives birth to imagination.

Henry David Thoreau

Look deep into Nature, and then you will understand everything better.

Albert Einstein

Nature does not hurry, yet everything is accomplished.

Lao Tzu

I dedicate this book to Charlie, my champion in life.

Contents

Encounters

Introduction

I have a small yard in Tucson, Arizona, full of surprise encounters, especially for a former New Yorker like myself. I'm used to a blander array of wild life—red robins, earthworms, and an occasional raccoon. Here I see small to midsize lizards and geckos that remind me of their prehistoric ancestors. They slither up and down the walls, signaling each other for dominance and for mating by pressing chests and front legs into push-ups. Hummingbirds, doves, and red and yellow-breasted wrens gather around the feeders with manic chirpings and territorial skirmishes. We have an owl and its mate that perch like sentinels on our chimney at night. Their hooting travels down through the fireplace and reverberates through the house. The roadrunners and hawks visit leaving us regurgitated piles of tiny bones and feathers. And there are comical moments, when a family of quail scoot by—one parent in the lead, the other tightly guarding the flank, their chicks moving like wisps of smoke between them; or one chick at a time trying to fly while the others seem to wait their turn under the careful watch of their parents.

In summer the heat seems to bleach the sky and mountains of color; summer monsoons bring in stacks of dark clouds, winds that smack everything around, and dangerous lightening. While the rains are a welcomed reprieve, the thirsty desert soaks it up immediately and heat descends again like a heavy curtain. At night these rains turn the desert caliche into mud, and toads burrow up through it, to mate in a frenzy and quack like ducks all over the yard. In early morning, they are still piled on top of each other; but by noon they've dug back down to rest until the night's bacchanal.

The sky and the Catalina Mountains form the backdrop for this yard, offering a constant interplay of light, shadow, color, and movement, depending upon time of day, season, and weather. Sunrises and sunsets paint the mountains amber and mauve. In all seasons, when the moon rises, the mountains form a majestic silhouette as far as the eye can see. Sometimes it feels to me like a sleeping behemoth just beyond our city.

I've written most of these poems after sunrise, before the heat envelops Tucson. In this contemplative space, writing poetry has been like casting a net and seeing what falls into it. My senses come alive from watching creatures mingle, mate, and forage; I do lots of planting and study what grows, blooms, and dies. All of it is metaphor for life. By mid-morning a poem has unfurled and my Muse slips away, satisfied. It's my hope that these poems will entice you to give yourself the gift of time and cast your own net.

Summer Writing

Thank You, Billy Collins

I'd like to say, never mind
it's been a dry summer,
barely a tease of monsoon
to wet earth's skin or
keep my writing juices flowing

but I read some Billy Collins today.
Like fog rolling out to sea,
my lethargy lifted.

He follows his curiosity,
let's it lead him by the hand
wonders what makes a robin
refuse to startle when
the front door is opened?

Such musings awaken
my own, and I venture out
from my dry corner
lick the tip of my pencil
for good luck
and write.

Breakfast with Champions

Their books spread open
like a meal, I had breakfast with
Natalie Goldberg, Mary Oliver,
and Lisa Koslow,

Natalie, the Buddhist, writes:
being in the "zone,"
surrounded by distraction,
gives "monkey mind"
branches for jumping on,
while "quiet mind"
sorts through what it must
to write.

Lisa, of Haiku, has this to say:
Trial and some error
not every effort is great
Magic comes and goes.

Mary with her poems about
mosquitoes, mushrooms, ants,
and the "blue forever sky,"
reminds me each is eternal,
that I, too, have a place
in this tapestry.

Cracked Open

This desert is a rough place
for a fair-skinned woman
who hates heat; but I write
in a hurry
before the jackhammer
cracks open the day.

I sip water and think
about my olive tree
that has no olives
but offers luscious shade;
how geckos can sleep, forage,
and mate in the summer sun;
how coyotes howl, taunt,
and tear apart their prey.

This desert is a rough place
for a thin-skinned woman
who hates heat; but I write
in a hurry
before the jackhammer
cracks open the day.

Presently Surprised

Today, while reading a poem,
I bumped into one of those trickster words
the eye can slice in half.
I went from nowhere to now here
and liked it better.

Nowhere
    is a grim, bully word
        especially if placed
            at the end of a sentence.

Now here
    is cheerful, offers possibility:
        You've just arrived,
            why not take a look around?

I'm left wondering:
what if we dropped this adverb
and just used now here
whenever nowhere came up?
Might we all be
presently surprised?

One Last Dance

It's a heat
that yanks me about
like an alligator
with prey in its snout.

Not yet I beg,
pen poised over paper
in this dawn of breezes,
pink and gold ribbons
for a sky.

There is
one dance left
for the Muse and I.

Encounters in
the Back Yard

Desert Weather

Yesterday the wind
whipped everything about
like a bully turning throats dry
and tongues so thick
you could taste the desert in your mouth.

Today's sky is an impossible blue
with a feather of a breeze
that stirs bush and branch.
Jasmine accept the nudge,
wave languidly from the trellis,
and the gardenia blossom
nods its head up and down,
releasing perfume.

All was transposed while I slept:
a wild wind grew tame,
air thick with sand that
painted my world putty,
now glistens like clean glass
as buds take another chance.

The Moment

In the night
a rose bud
clings to a stem
petals fist tight
against the chill.
Fuller, rounder
next morning,
a moment will come
when it opens,
petals stretching
into a back bend
leaving its stamp of
perfume and color
on the world.

Steward of the Bird Bath

What's up with the bird bath?
Why no takers
fanning wet wings,
dipping beaks,
gifting me their thirsty chirpings?

Too much sand and grit
or a hint of green slime
growing where it shouldn't?

I am the steward of
this tiny wet world.
It is my job to clean
and wipe away anything
that doesn't belong.

So I scoop out leaves,
sponge away what's green,
bring hose to rim, re-fill
and wait.

They return,
reminding me that
attention to a simple bird bath
is a lesson in stewardship.

A Sweeping Practice

Imagine this simple practice:
with broom in hand
look down at the ground,
mindfully sweep
whatever is there:
dust, feather,
pod, bug
and know you
may have missed
a thing or two;
that even a breeze
can scatter
your best efforts.
Sure, you can grouse
about that or
begin again,
to guide the broom
toward whatever
is there.

Hermaphrodite

Hibiscus blossom

opens

crimson petals

unfold,

swoon

like girls in love,

in their center

red pistals rise

confident as cocks

ringed with yellow stamen

droplets of semen

gracing

their

tips.

Cardinal

A red-orange flame
that dances and sings
in the olive tree?

This is a home to
dull gray doves and
sun bleached lizards.

You bright rascal!
You punctuate my world,
awaken urges,
make me giddy.

Night Marauders

A splash of buttery marigolds,
crimson geraniums, purple petunias
trail over the rim of the pot,
to welcome visitors.

They are a tasty meal
for night marauders –
rabbits, squirrels, birds,
and the ever industrious
pack rat.

I try other species
that come from the nursery
like eager toddlers,
shoots and petals ready
to play in the sun.

I sprinkle cayenne pepper
and prayer among the petals.

Soon frost takes its own bite.
My prodigies lose color,
bend over and die. Only then,
will I surrender to
a rubber welcome mat.

Two Winds

Last night the wind thrashed
against the walls of my house,
pushed under roof tiles with a meanness,
rattled window frames, and yanked me
shaking from a dream:

I was somewhere deep inside Africa,
a refugee child in my arms,
delicate lips blistered, belly swollen hard with hunger.
Outside the flimsy shelter of our tent
a wind howled, gathered into a battering ram of sand,
while ten year old conscripts with rifles and machetes
sat around in a circle smoking cigarettes.

From last night's mayhem,
there are plastic chairs strewn about our yard,
seat cushions bob in the swimming pool like castaways;
but it is the bushes that had neatly climbed the walls -
they are bent and broken
and I am reminded that such dreams
are indeed another reality.

Ode to My Olive Tree

I love your three trunks
old and sturdy as crones
branches like veins
with life coursing through them
giving rise to green oval leaves.

Shade is plentiful under
your canopy,
hummingbirds make their
thimble nests among the leaves,
hawks, wrens, and doves
pass in and out all day
creating a cacophony of warbles,
cluckings, and chirpings.

I hang chimes and bells
from your branches,
a tinkle of notes that reverberate
forming singular melodies
that never repeat.

A crystal dangles from a branch
casting rainbows on a wall or leaf
in the lemony light and soft breeze
of late afternoon.

Best of all
you drop your leaves
for me to sweep each morning,
and, like a monk in an abbey,
I bow to this practice
of stewardship.

Little Brown Bat

Upside down and dangling
like a handkerchief
from the light fixture.
Are you trapped,
sleeping, or dead?

I fear waving the broom
to release or wake you.
As you are bound by daylight
so am I by old wives tales of
bats tangled in hair.

You gorge on a thousand insects
in one hour, sucking and chewing
your body the size of my thumb,
but on my back porch primordial fear
runs through my veins when I see you.

I put on the Brandenburg Concerto
to calm us both down,
step beneath you to clean up
droplets of shit and blood red urine,
traces of your night marauding
for crickets, mosquitoes, and moths.

Don't kill it, I tell my husband,
who thankfully has little hair.
Just coax it gently with the broom.
He does and little brown bat
drops to the ground
like a dead leaf, finished
for the season.

Doggie Lessons

The Day We Both Turned 70

Stretching my joints
with long strides,
Zena, prances ahead
nose twitching with the scent
of coyote and dog poop.

Her ears flap and bounce
like a happy child's hands,
the soft spot between them
where I press my face -
it tempts me now, but, at seventy,
she and I must not squander
precious momentum.

Suddenly she slows to a stop,
leash slips to the ground.
I test with a knee against her rump –
a gentle coax, but she roots firmly
like an old mesquite the wind
cannot push around.

I bend to pull her – feel a twinge
in my fourth lumbar. Okay, I say,
no shame in retreat.
Seventy gives us both the privilege
to turn toward home.

I smile, for now there is
a spring in her gait, she's
going home. For me,
a new ease with acceptance.

Patience

This morning I looked closely
at my dog's nose:
black as ink, two perfect holes
separated by a tender crease
with a delicate quiver
of nostrils anticipating
the familiar pleasure
of licking egg salad from the dish.

She sits at attention
and I bend for an even closer look at her,
doggie breath covering my face
like a warm damp cloth.

Her patience reminds me of
what it means
to wait for what you truly love:
you can whine, woof, or wiggle
into a frenzy, or
sit patiently on your haunches
until it's offered to you.

Unconditional Love

In a licking frenzy
Zena's tongue slides around
the inside of the cup
egg salad all over her nose.

Sometimes our pleasures are reciprocal:
Raking my fingers through her thick fur
feeling her wet nose, like a tear drop
on mine, grazing the tips of her eyelashes
as I wipe away sleepers, dozing off
to her deep doggie sighs beside me.

I was lazy and didn't
take her for a walk this morning
told myself it was too hot -
but she waited patiently by the gate
tail wagging. Sequestering myself
in the shade, she finally joined me
wedging her nose between my knees
ears waiting for my gentle tug and scratch.

There is no other being in my life
offering such acceptance
and limitless affection.
Were she family, friend, or lover,
I would have to do a better job
reciprocating.

Next time, I shall walk her in the heat -
a modest human sacrifice for a dog
that gives lessons in unconditional love.

Husband

On Our 48th Wedding Anniversary

It occurred to me
we might renew our
vows that night,
pledge how we'd
love the other with
more vigor.

I watched you
chew and swallow
your food,
remembered
the old hunger
of our mouths,
slow kisses,
urgency of tongues
probing for what wanted
to be consumed.

You sipped your drink,
and I waited
for a romantic morsel,
something sexy, savory
to fill this unannounced
craving for you!

Pairings

Today a pair of doves
sit on the wall in our yard,
one grooming the other
with little pecks between
feathers. They fly
to the bird bath,
dip beaks and drink,
go back to the wall
and snooze.

This summer
we celebrated
our 49th anniversary.
and flew to Africa.
We held hands
in the back of jeeps,
dozed in each other's arms
on dusty rides back to camp.
Others noticed this touching,
wanted to know our secret
for staying married.

All I can think of
is that years have burnished us
to a warm, glossy finish.
Like the doves,
we each dip into life, drink our fill,
and are willing to scratch
the other's back
when there's an itch.

Who's the Pragmatist?

When someone asked:
What's the secret
to your long marriage?
You laughed and said:
A long leash for each.

No, it's my unlimited access
to the soft curls on your chest,
the feel of your knees searching
for the crease behind mine,
the tender dampness of your skin
in the morning.

Truth is,
I was a romantic,
you the pragmatist,
with hideouts where
pass words did not exist.

Now, I know how to
pace in those shadows,
have figured out why
it's worth the wait.

Consensual

Might start my morning
under the covers
reading poetry, while
Zena paws you awake
for food and exercise.

We eat breakfast together.
You, organized at the stove,
a mug of sweetened coffee
waiting for me. Sweet man.
I munch a piece of toast,
feel the pull back to bed,
watch you eat in silence,
your mind on what's next.

Lately, we refill our mugs,
take them to the couch,
sit near one another, talk.
It's a small new intimacy.
Promising, like a wild flower.

Beyond the Yard

Roadrunner

Your combed feathered form
stands before me,
long regal neck, a beak
that swallows rattlesnakes.

Am I imagining this,
or do we size one another up?
Lips puckered, I make
swooshing sounds,
click tongue against the roof
of my mouth to entice you.

You fix me with a beady stare,
eyes yellow and sly,
puff out your Mohawk crown,
take a few staccato steps.

I continue my vocal gymnastics,
unaccustomed to such mimicry,
cough and sputter, break away
to look for a tissue.

Meanwhile, you've lost interest,
disappear into a prickly canopy
of mesquite, where I cannot follow.

Moon

She is your moon and mine
what we have in common,
despite all that separates us
beneath her light.

Night after night
she steps out on stage
revealing a little more of herself
like a seasoned stripper,
she coaxes and teases
until we bathe in her blunt round whiteness.

She is everyone's moon,
even the little child in Sudan
who sits on a patch of crusty moonlit earth,
a stick his only weapon against mindless slaughter;
even the sick rapist hunched over his steering wheel,
surveying the moonlit parking lot for prey.

And over centuries
women have whirled wildly, chanted,
beaten drums as they dig into earth's belly,
to bury their placentas and monthly blood
under her canopy of light.

With soothing predictability
she tugs at ocean floors,
rules the tides,
and draws back the covers that bathe our earth,
pulls it toward her bosom and releases.

Crackerman

Driving to book club
thinking about Karma,
I turn up the radio
send Chopin
into the streets.

Next to me
in a convertible
base pounding,
a shirtless man howls
to Garth Brooks.

In a past life,
he might have been
a mystic and I,
some woman's
crackerman.

Timing

How does the dove
convince its partner
to make dove-love
inside that bush?

How does my scapular
take over for a
broken clavicle,
so I have one good hand
to turn pages?

How does the mind know
when it's full
and pen
must come to paper,
scatter words
like seeds?

Therapist

Once I was a shaky soul
in a waiting room
with hope that
fifty minutes
would still
my trembling.

Now I lean in
to hold your
fear and shame,
bullies that press
against the tender
parts of you.

Arab and Jew

First time
I saw a mountain of a woman
in an orange caftan,
sandals on sun cracked feet.
A white kafiyah framed
the face, eyes peeping out
from folds of skin.

The second time
I said good morning.
she nodded her head, smiled
so shyly I found myself
imagining her a grandmother
like me snipping mint for tea
but whispering prayers
to Allah.

Perhaps she has a jihadist
grandson, body coiled
to throw a bomb at a bus
or maybe she just washes
her floors with vinegar
like I do.

The last time,
she was squatting near the walkway.
Peeing under that tent or sick?
She looked calmly at me,
and I knew: this is how you rest.

Reminders

I slide the plate with toast and eggs
across the table to you.
It's a clean sound, counterpoint
to the crunch of newspaper
you turn and fold.

I avert my eyes from the headlines and listen for
the sip of coffee passing over your lips.
These days I thrive on familiarity,
eschew bad news.

Hummingbird alights on the feeder with a swoosh.
Finches twirp and click as they pick at seeds.
Zena answers whoof to something wild in the wash below.
There's a lazy clang of wood on metal as breeze stirs our wind chime.

Your fingers idly drum on the table as you read the Arizona Star:
A three year old drowned yesterday in the family's swimming pool.
The family left the gate unlocked.

A singular breath - mine or yours – sucked in and released.
When was the last time we locked our pool gate?
It stands ajar, rust on the latch.

Our pool looks benignly inviting
as the morning unfolds and the heat builds.
In a few hours I will do my water aerobics,
splash about with a spiderman kick board
and colored noodles reserved
for our grandchildren's visits.
Grown up now, all except
the three year old.

Lucas

It's not yet 8 a.m.
and I hear the basketball
thumpity thump thump
next door.

Lucas is his name.
Eleven with a head of hair
thick and wild around his handsome face.
Doesn't get along with his father.
Parents are divorced.

Lucas has a sister too,
a few years older,
lots of makeup and an attitude
of whatever, duh.
She and her mother fight
but it's Lucas
who sounds a note of sadness
with his lonely dribbling of the basketball.
I want to call over the wall to him:
I hear you Lucas.

Half Connected

I stare out at my back wall and
see the bouncing tops of heads,
hear the crunch of sneakers on gravel,
and catch breathless snippets of
joggers on cell phones.

But what about these
half connections
when the whole person is there
seated across the table,
and we still gaze down
at our devices?

Sometimes I call over the wall
shout a hearty good morning
to a bobbing baseball cap
or a swinging pony tail just
to break the trance.

My Widowed Friend

Lisa writes of *silent solitude*
a space not filled or wall-papered
with music or conversation.
I imagine it often leads to
the writing of her next Haiku.

She could be banging pot lids
slamming doors as a silent howl of loneliness
gathers in her belly but instead

she often stretches out
with a book across her chest
meaning to read but dozing off
letting time drift,
being gentle with herself.

She drives home alone
from dinner with friends,
her car carefully maintained
for safety and reliability
music stations set for her own enjoyment,
body easing behind the wheel,
seat adjusted to her body.

She is a competent woman
able to bend time into slotted endeavors;
but it is the Haiku, written daily
as one might drop an anchor,
that steadies her, helps her
chart the course of her life.

Searching for Rumi

This morning I went looking
for my Rumi book,
a gift from a friend,
when I needed
a friend.

The book is gone,
every shelf searched
and searched again...
cannot imagine giving
this gift away.

My friend is gone too,
moved to another state,
contact stretched so thin,
that one day it simply disappeared.

Rumi gone,
my friend gone,
and what remains
is the possibility of
another book, another friend
or acceptance of temporary gifts.

Homeless Reader

All I know about this man
is that he is a reader
and persistent:
shows up, rain or shine,
every day, same place
squats by the curb, arms lined
with tattoos, one hand holding
a book behind the cardboard sign
Homeless/ Broke/ Please Help

He could have ear buds
with music thrumming,
that might obliterate
the boredom of waiting
for do-gooders
with loose change

but instead he reads,
eyes cast down to the print
away from pitying stares,
perhaps conjuring a place
beyond this patch of concrete.

At the Gym

A young woman
with Downe Syndrome
steps on the treadmill,
thighs puckered,
a weggie in her shorts
but she doesn't care
swings her booty
and ponytail
for the guy
in *Footloose*.

A second screen
has a young,
talk show host
with perky breasts
and gravitas.
She asks:
"Is it better to endure
the pain of a Brazilian wax
or let those curly clusters
hang out?"

At seventy, I'm
pedaling nice 'n easy,
the bike reclines,
curly clusters
have disappeared,
Now I'm a large in tights.
I vote with booty girl.
Let it all hang out.

Endings

Spare Me Your Goodbyes

Like a queen you reigned
from your bed
I cleaned and straightened
while you slept,
put everything in arm's reach
including my love.

I, your hand-maiden,
adjusted pillows
behind your head,
anointed cracked skin
with cream and oils,
served you smoothies
with crushed ice
and dollops of ice cream.

We did not speak even once
of what was to come. Yet,
one day you asked me
to spread out your jewelry,
put pins, rings, necklaces,
into baggies labeled
for relatives and friends.

I wanted to end this charade,
curl up next to you
with my memories
of your pearls and ruby necklace
mark our best times
as mother and daughter
in laughter and tears
that would wash us clean,
but your eyes said, please
spare me your goodbyes.

Too Late

It's been hard to write the *Goodbye* chapter
    about Mom dying in the yellow bedroom
        that smell of Pond's Cold Cream
           how I ran into her bathroom

when mortuary attendants entered,
    gurney and body bag between them
        turning everything final.

I listened for the sound of rubber
    tugged and folded around her body,
        prayed they'd lift her with reverence
           due their mothers

Then came the final click of zipper's teeth
    and it was too late to tell them
        this would not be her way to leave

    Please instead . . .

cover her with the soft blanket from her bed
    gather strands of hair into a pink ribbon,
        let it peep out from the blanket's edge
           as her final wink to life.

My Mother's Gold Chain

I wear your gold chain
around my neck.
It rests on my freckled skin
as it did yours
until the hour after
you took your last breath
and they told me
to remove your jewelry.

There is one link that refuses
to obey – is twisted,
and I am tempted to set it straight
but it reminds me of our relationship
with its imperfections, a reminder
for me to forgive and love you
unconditionally.

I wish you could see
how your great-granddaughter
curls her little fingers around it
pulls it toward her mouth
and says "mine".

One day it will be hers
and she might notice
the link that bends the other way,
how it does not alter
the beauty of the chain.

Prose Poem for My Father

On our walks after Sabbath services you stopped to
trace the veins of a leaf and point to bees in a rose
bush. You said: This is the Creator's handiwork.
We are a hiccup in his universe. Your hand on the
back of my neck, I felt so willing to let you steer me
down suburban streets and through my life.

But the inevitable happened: boys on my radar, the
ping and swing of Dick Clark's *American Bandstand.*
You made a big mistake by calling it "garbage." I
found excuses not to go to services with you, began
to steal Mom's cigarettes, stuff my bra for more
cleavage. Later, I flung feminism against your religion.
Lines were drawn. You wouldn't give an inch. Said:
We are a hiccup in His universe. I swear you prayed
even harder, pulled religion around you like an overcoat.

But when you were dying, I came to Florida, told you
that once you were the center of my universe. Not sure
you even heard me. Your body was as small as a boy's,
breath a whisper. The prayer book rested on your lap,
the spine cracked from being held open against your
heart for so many years. I cradled it in my hands and
thought maybe life is God's version of a riddle. Your
lips moved soundlessly as I recited prayers we once
said together on Sabbath mornings when you stopped
to trace veins in a leaf and point to bees in a rose bush.

Notes from Your Encounters

Made in the USA
Las Vegas, NV
27 August 2022

54135896R00069